Would
You
Rather
Book
for Teens
AF482932

Are you ready to face the weirdest, funniest, and downright toughest "Would You Rather" questions ever?

From magical pets to crazy superpowers, food choices that will make you cringe, and laugh-out-loud challenges, this book has it all! Perfect for sleepovers, road trips, parties, or just hanging out with friends, every page will leave you wondering, "What would I choose?!"

Get ready to make impossible decisions, take on silly dares, and discover what your choices say about you. You might be surprised by the answers you and your friends come up with — but one thing's for sure: you'll be laughing the whole way through!

So… Would You Rather Start Now or Miss Out on All the Fun?

Open the book, make your choice, and let the adventure begin!

WOULD YOU RATHER

Only be able to whisper

or

Only be able to shout

?

WOULD YOU RATHER

Be the world's best singer

or

Be the world's best scientist

?

WOULD YOU RATHER

Have a pet dragon

or

Have a pet unicorn

?

WOULD YOU RATHER

Only be able to whisper

or

Only be able to shout

?

WOULD YOU RATHER

Be the world's best singer

or

Be the world's best scientist

?

WOULD YOU RATHER

Have a pet dragon

or

Have a pet unicorn

?

WOULD YOU RATHER

Be able to fly

or

Be able to time travel

?

WOULD YOU RATHER

Live without air conditioning

or

Live without heating

?

WOULD YOU RATHER

Be cursed to live forever

or

Be cursed to die young

?

WOULD YOU RATHER

Always have your food raw

or

Always have your food very

?

WOULD YOU RATHER

Be vegetarian

or

Never have any fruits or
vegetables again

?

WOULD YOU RATHER

Eat broccoli-chip cookies

or

Eat avocado ice cream

?

WOULD YOU RATHER

Never have hot food again
or
Never have cold food again
?

WOULD YOU RATHER

Be able to fly
or
Be able to time travel
?

WOULD YOU RATHER

Always have bad breath
or
Always smell like stinky feet
?

WOULD YOU RATHER

Fight 1000 ant-sized bulls

or

Fight one bull-sized ant

?

WOULD YOU RATHER

Use your BFF's used toothbrush

or

Use your BFF's dirty underwear

?

WOULD YOU RATHER

Always have an eyelash in your eye

or

Always have spinach between your teeth

?

WOULD YOU RATHER

Never forget anything again

or

Never remember anything again

?

WOULD YOU RATHER

Have the lights
on or off
in a room full of poisonous snakes

?

WOULD YOU RATHER

Wake up in your underwear at school

or

Wake up naked in a forest far away
from home

?

WOULD YOU RATHER

Be able to read minds
or
Be able to control minds
?

WOULD YOU RATHER

Give up sugar for a year
or
Give up your phone for a month
?

WOULD YOU RATHER

Be chased by a pack of wolves
or
Be chased by a herd of zombies
?

WOULD YOU RATHER
Spend a night in a graveyard
or
Spend a night in a haunted house
?

WOULD YOU RATHER
Drink soapy water
or
Drink muddy water
?

WOULD YOU RATHER
Drink one glass of rotten milk
or
Drink one decilitre of blood
?

WOULD YOU RATHER
Always wear shoes two sizes
too small
or
Always wear shoes five sizes
too big
?

WOULD YOU RATHER
Have antennas
or
Have a tail
?

WOULD YOU RATHER
Never get sick again
or
Never get hurt again
?

WOULD YOU RATHER

Be a police officer

or

Be a firefighter

?

WOULD YOU RATHER

Always feel like you have
to sneeze

or

Always have the hiccoughs

?

WOULD YOU RATHER

Be the strongest person in
the world
or
Be the smartest person in
the world

?

WOULD YOU RATHER

Never have to sleep again
or
Never have to eat again
?

WOULD YOU RATHER

Be able to fly for a day
or
Be invisible for a day
?

WOULD YOU RATHER

Be able to understand animals
or
Have animals understand you
?

WOULD YOU RATHER

Be able to control water

or

Be able to control fire

?

WOULD YOU RATHER

Be as small as an ant

or

Be as large as a giant

?

WOULD YOU RATHER

Never have homework again

or

Do homework every day,
but getting paid for it

?

WOULD YOU RATHER

Always sew your own clothes

or

Always grow your own food

?

WOULD YOU RATHER

Be poor but live in a mansion

or

Be rich but live in a tent

?

WOULD YOU RATHER

Lie to your BFF to protect
their feelings

or

Tell them the truth and hurt them

?

WOULD YOU RATHER

Lose all your family's money

or

Lose all your family's pictures and memorable items

?

WOULD YOU RATHER

Receive a gift hand-made with love by your BFF

or

Receive an expensive store-bought gift from a stranger

?

WOULD YOU RATHER

Smell amazing all the time

or

Look amazing all the time

?

WOULD YOU RATHER

Buy 5 items you don't want every time you go to the store

or

Always forget one thing on your shopping list

?

WOULD YOU RATHER

Not shower for two weeks

or

Not brush your teeth for two weeks

?

WOULD YOU RATHER

Live in a city where no one knows you

or

Live in a city where everyone knows you

?

WOULD YOU RATHER

Date someone 12 years older
than you

or

Date someone 4 years younger
than you

?

WOULD YOU RATHER

Never be able to turn the lights
on in your room

or

Never be able to turn the lights
off in your room

?

WOULD YOU RATHER

Be super famous and never have
any privacy

or

Be a hermit and never have
company

?

WOULD YOU RATHER
Be a giant mouse
or
A tiny elephant
?

WOULD YOU RATHER
Never be able to close your eyes
or
Never be able to close your mouth
?

WOULD YOU RATHER
Never stop singing
or
Never stop dancing
?

WOULD YOU RATHER

Spend the rest of your life indoors

or

Spend the rest of your life outdoors

?

WOULD YOU RATHER

Wear clown shoes for a month

or

Wear a clown nose for a month

?

WOULD YOU RATHER

Have no sense of smell

or

Have a super strong sense of smell

?

WOULD YOU RATHER

Have a giant nose

or

Have a giant mouth

?

WOULD YOU RATHER

Have to shout "THAT'S ME!" every
time someone says your name

or

Never have anyone knowing
your name again

?

WOULD YOU RATHER

Be a poor genious

or

Be rich and dumb

?

WOULD YOU RATHER

Have to sing every time
you hear music
or
Have to dance every time
you hear music
?

WOULD YOU RATHER

Only speak in a
high-pitched voice
or
Only speak in rhyme
?

WOULD YOU RATHER

Never have anyone laugh at
your jokes
or
Never find anything funny again
?

WOULD YOU RATHER

Have a giant unibrow

or

Have your back covered
in long hair

?

WOULD YOU RATHER

Have a constant itch

or

Have a constant headache

?

WOULD YOU RATHER

Be the main character in a
scary movie

or

Be the main character in a
romantic comedy

?

WOULD YOU RATHER

Find true love
or
Win a million dollars

?

WOULD YOU RATHER

Have to listen to music 24/7
or
Never hear music again

?

WOULD YOU RATHER

Be stranded on a desert island
with your worst enemy
or
Be stranded on a desert island
all alone

?

WOULD YOU RATHER

Be a famous expert in one thing only

or

Know a little about everything

?

WOULD YOU RATHER

Never touch anything electronic again

or

Never touch another human again

?

WOULD YOU RATHER

Have a bad nightmare three times a week for the rest of your life

or

Never be able to dream again

?

WOULD YOU RATHER

Know who you will marry

or

When you will get married

?

WOULD YOU RATHER

Know how you will die

or

Know when you will die

?

WOULD YOU RATHER

Go a year without music

or

Go a year without movies and TV

?

WOULD YOU RATHER

Get straight A's in school but never be invited to parties

or

Be invited to every party but only get F's in school

?

WOULD YOU RATHER

Live in an amusement park

or

Live in a zoo

?

WOULD YOU RATHER

Only have one best friend

or

Only have 100 surface level friends

?

WOULD YOU RATHER

Be annoyingly confident

or

Be extremely shy

?

WOULD YOU RATHER

Be good looking and stupid

or

Be ugly and very intelligent

?

WOULD YOU RATHER

Be able to only text with emojis

or

Not being able to text at all

?

WOULD YOU RATHER

Lose all your past memories

or

Never make another

new memory

?

WOULD YOU RATHER

Be an amazing artist

or

Be a genious mathematician

?

WOULD YOU RATHER

Go to any restaurant

for free forever

or

Go to any theme park

for free forever

?

WOULD YOU RATHER

Be a sketchy person who works for
an honest company
or
Be an honest person who works for a
sketchy company
?

WOULD YOU RATHER

Give up all drinks except water
or
Never have water again
?

WOULD YOU RATHER

Have all your clothes be 6 sizes
too big
or
Have all your clothes be 2 sizes
too small
?

WOULD YOU RATHER

Lose your sense of taste
or
Lose your sense of smell
?

WOULD YOU RATHER

Have the ability to read minds
or
Have the ability to see the future
?

WOULD YOU RATHER

Have a permanent splinter in
your foot
or
Have a permanently itchy
mosquito bite
?

WOULD YOU RATHER

Always be 30 minutes late
or
Always be two hours early
?

WOULD YOU RATHER

Be able to see the future
or
Be able to change the past
?

WOULD YOU RATHER

Only charge your phone
once a week
or
Have no camera on your phone
?

WOULD YOU RATHER

Only be able to watch movies starring
The Rock

or

Only be able to watch movies in foreign
languagesand without subtitles

?

WOULD YOU RATHER

Win Idol

or

Win Masterchef

?

WOULD YOU RATHER

Switch closets with a parent

or

Only wear clothes chosen by a
grandparent

?

WOULD YOU RATHER
Have a famous family member
or
Be the famous family member
?

WOULD YOU RATHER
Have all your meals amazing in a
luxury restaurant, but all alone
or
Have all your meals mediocre, but at
home with your family
?

WOULD YOU RATHER
Wear winter clothes all year long
or
Wear summer clothes all year long
?

WOULD YOU RATHER

Always only use dog shampoo

or

Never cut your toenails

?

WOULD YOU RATHER

Always fart really loud in public,
but with no smell

or

Always smell like fart in public

?

WOULD YOU RATHER

Always burp out loud in public

or

Always have sweat stains under
your arms

?

WOULD YOU RATHER

Be your class'substitute teacher for a
day
or
Have your parents be your class'
substitute teachers for a day
?

WOULD YOU RATHER

Have school 3 days a week for 12
hours
or
Have school 6 days a week for 6 hours
?

WOULD YOU RATHER

Sing in front of your whole school
or
Compete in a spelling bee in front
of your whole school

?

WOULD YOU RATHER
Have all your food covered in
spicy chili peppers
or
Have all your food covered in sugar
?

WOULD YOU RATHER
Break everything you touch
or
Never touch anything with your
hands again
?

WOULD YOU RATHER
Be your family's pet dog
or
Be a wild fox
?

WOULD YOU RATHER

Have super strength
or
Have super hearing
?

WOULD YOU RATHER

Make a lot of money but hate your job
or
Make below average but love your job
?

WOULD YOU RATHER

Be really good at synchronised
swimming
or
Be really good at
Irish step dancing
?

WOULD YOU RATHER

Be turned down for a dance by someone you like

or

Dance with someone you don't like

?

WOULD YOU RATHER

Go on a date with someone who can't remember your name

or

Go on a date with someone who accidentally calls you by their ex's name

?

WOULD YOU RATHER

Get diarrhea on a first date

or

Have your parents join you on a first date

?

WOULD YOU RATHER

Date someone gorgeous but boring

or

Date someone ugly but hilarious

?

WOULD YOU RATHER

Be Deadpool

or

Be Ironman

?

WOULD YOU RATHER

Have dinner with Shakespeare

or

Have dinner with Astrid Lindgren

?

WOULD YOU RATHER

Be covered head-to-toe in tattoos

or

Be covered head-to-toe in hair

?

WOULD YOU RATHER

Travel to another dimension

or

Travel to another planet

?

WOULD YOU RATHER

Stop using all paper products

or

Stop using all plastic products

?

WOULD YOU RATHER

Marry a stranger
or
Never get married at all
?

WOULD YOU RATHER

Break the camera on your phone
or
Break the screen on your phone
?

WOULD YOU RATHER

Not be able to feel anything
or
Be super sensitive to all touch
?

WOULD YOU RATHER

Be a ghost

or

Be a zombie

?

WOULD YOU RATHER

Have photographic memory

or

Be able to hear colours

?

WOULD YOU RATHER

Live without plumbing

or

Live without electricity

?

WOULD YOU RATHER

Perform brain surgery on someone
or
Perform heart surgery on someone

?

WOULD YOU RATHER

Walk barefoot over hot coals
or
Walk barefoot over Lego-bricks

?

WOULD YOU RATHER

Sound like a sheep when you laugh
or
Sound like an elephant when
you cry

?

WOULD YOU RATHER

Trip and fall bad in front of
your crush

or

Throw up in front of your crush

?

WOULD YOU RATHER

Find a band-aid in your food

or

Find someone's fake nail
in your food

?

WOULD YOU RATHER

Accidentally send an embarrassing
picture to your teacher

or

Accidentally send an embarrassing
picture to your grandmother

?

WOULD YOU RATHER

Be extremely ticklish

or

Be extremely sensitive to noise

?

WOULD YOU RATHER

Have no eyebrows

or

Have no fingernails

?

WOULD YOU RATHER

Always be sweaty

or

Always be cold

?

WOULD YOU RATHER

Kiss someone you like when you
have bad breath
or
Never kiss them at all
?

WOULD YOU RATHER

Live together with a centaur
or
Live together with a mermaid
?

WOULD YOU RATHER

Lose a hand
or
Lose a foot
?

WOULD YOU RATHER

Be terrified of pillows

or

Be terrified of blankets

?

WOULD YOU RATHER

Get flushed down the toilet

or

Get thrown in the trash

?

WOULD YOU RATHER

Be stuck as a teen forever

or

Skip the teen years of your life

?

WOULD YOU RATHER

Have your hair turn grey
or
Dye your hair bright pink

?

WOULD YOU RATHER

Watch a movie with no sound
or
Listen to a movie with no picture

?

WOULD YOU RATHER

Get banned from TikTok
or
Get banned from Snapchat

?

WOULD YOU RATHER

Get caught starting a mean rumor
about your BFF
or
Have a mean rumor started
about you
?

WOULD YOU RATHER

Be the teacher's pet
or
Be the class clown
?

WOULD YOU RATHER

Be grounded for a month
or
Not being welcome home
for a month
?

WOULD YOU RATHER

Always wear shoes two sizes
too big
or
Two sizes too small
?

WOULD YOU RATHER

Have bangs that always cover
your eyes
or
Glasses that constantly slip
down
?

WOULD YOU RATHER

Have the superpower of invisibility
but only in the dark
or the ability to fly but only one
meter high
?

WOULD YOU RATHER

Have every selfie turn out blurry
or
Always have a weird face in
photos

?

WOULD YOU RATHER

Have three extra fingers
or
One extra leg

?

WOULD YOU RATHER

Wear mismatched socks every
day
or
Wear one shoe without an insole

?

WOULD YOU RATHER

Wear clothes that are always one
size too big
or
One size too small

?

WOULD YOU RATHER

Have an endless supply of ice
cream
or
An endless supply of fries

?

WOULD YOU RATHER

Have eyebrows that are half as
long
or
Twice as thick

?

WOULD YOU RATHER

Walk around all day with a leaf
stuck to your forehead
or
With sticky gel on your hands

?

WOULD YOU RATHER

Have rainbow-colored hair
or
Perpetually messy hair

?

WOULD YOU RATHER

Have lips that glow in the dark
or
Nails that change color every hour

?

WOULD YOU RATHER

Be able to talk to trees
or
Understand what fish are thinking

?

WOULD YOU RATHER

Spend a week without your phone
or
A week without internet

?

WOULD YOU RATHER

Have a robot that always cleans up
after you
or
An assistant who always does your
homework

?

WOULD YOU RATHER

Always wear neon-colored clothes
or
Only wear gray

?

WOULD YOU RATHER

Be able to rewind time by 10
seconds
or
Skip forward 10 minutes

?

WOULD YOU RATHER

Wear the same outfit every day
or
Nave a different, uncomfortable
outfit every day

?

WOULD YOU RATHER

Be able to read animals' minds
or
Speak every language in the world
?

WOULD YOU RATHER

Never watch your favorite show again
or
Never listen to your favorite song again
?

WOULD YOU RATHER

Have star-shaped teeth
or
A heart-shaped tongue
?

WOULD YOU RATHER

Start every conversation with a joke
or
End every goodbye with a weird
dance
?

WOULD YOU RATHER

Never eat pizza again

or

Never eat ice cream again
?

WOULD YOU RATHER

Have perpetually cold hands

or

Perpetually sweaty hands
?

WOULD YOU RATHER

Have a new hairstyle every day

or

A new pair of shoes every day

?

WOULD YOU RATHER

Be ignored by everyone

or

Have everyone stare at you constantly

?

WOULD YOU RATHER

Watch every movie with a sad ending

or

Every movie with a funny ending

?

WOULD YOU RATHER

Have hair that's always wet

or

Clothes that are always a bit tight

?

WOULD YOU RATHER

Never leave the house without an umbrella

or

Always have a straw hat with you

?

WOULD YOU RATHER

Wear a neon pink shirt for a month

or

Neon green pants for a month

?

WOULD YOU RATHER

Always have internet but no games

or

Always have games but no internet

?

WOULD YOU RATHER

Paint your room a new color every
month

or

Have walls made of mirrors

?

WOULD YOU RATHER

Wear the same pair of shoes forever

or

A new, weird pair every day

?

FUN CHALLENGES

Would You Rather

Question: "Have a pet dragon or have a pet unicorn?"

Challenge:

If you chose the dragon – make your best dragon face and try to let out a "fiery" roar!

If you chose the unicorn – run around the room, pretending to flick a magical unicorn tail!

Would You Rather

Question: "Eat only spaghetti with no sauce or only eat sandwiches with no bread?"

Challenge:

If you chose spaghetti – pretend to slurp invisible noodles as loudly as you can!

If you chose sandwiches – mime eating the most delicious "sandwich" you can imagine (without the bread, of course!).

FUN CHALLENGES

Would You Rather

Question: "Be able to fly or be able to time travel?"

Challenge:

If you chose flying – flap your arms like wings and pretend to fly around the room for 30 seconds!

If you chose time travel – describe where and when you would go if you could time travel, and why!

Would You Rather

Question: "Have a permanent clown nose or permanent clown shoes?"

Challenge:

If you chose the clown nose – make three silly faces that show off your "clown personality."

If you chose the clown shoes – walk around the room in exaggerated, giant clown steps

FUN CHALLENGES

Would You Rather

Question: "Live without air conditioning or live without heating?"

Challenge:

If you chose no air conditioning – imagine you're in the hottest place you know, and act out how you would cool yourself down!

If you chose no heating – show how you would keep warm in the middle of winter without any heat!

Would You Rather

Question: "Be able to teleport anywhere or be able to become invisible?"

Challenge:

If you chose teleporting – choose a random spot in the room and "teleport" there with a dramatic pose!

If you chose invisibility – try to "hide" by blending in with something in the room (like standing next to a wall or covering yourself with a pillow).

FUN CHALLENGES

Would You Rather

Question: "Be able to talk to animals or be able to speak every language in the world?"

Challenge:

If you chose talking to animals – imitate the sound of your favorite animal for 10 seconds and see if anyone can guess it!

If you chose speaking every language – say "hello" in as many languages as you know, or make up your own greeting and teach it to others!

Would You Rather

Question: "Only be able to eat breakfast food for the rest of your life or only be able to eat dessert?"

Challenge:

If you chose breakfast – describe the ultimate breakfast you'd eat every day if you could.

If you chose dessert – pretend to eat an imaginary ice cream cone and describe the most ridiculous flavor combinations you can think of.

FUN CHALLENGES

Would You Rather

Question: "Have a magical power to freeze time or a power to read minds?"

Challenge:

If you chose freezing time – freeze in place like a statue for 15 seconds without moving a muscle!

If you chose reading minds – pretend to read someone's mind in the room and make a funny guess about what they're thinking!

Would You Rather

Question: "Have hair that changes color based on your mood or shoes that change style every hour?"

Challenge:

If you chose mood-hair – describe what color your hair would be right now based on your mood.

If you chose style-changing shoes – act out what it would be like to realize your shoes suddenly changed into roller skates!

FUN CHALLENGES

Would You Rather

Question: "Have to dance whenever you hear music or have to sing along to every song you hear?"

Challenge:

If you chose dancing – show off your best dance moves for 10 seconds to imaginary music!

If you chose singing – sing the first line of your favorite song as loudly and enthusiastically as you can!

Would You Rather

Question: "Be able to understand what animals are saying or be able to talk to plants?"

Challenge:

If you chose animals – choose an animal and make up a funny sentence you think it would say.

If you chose plants – have a short "conversation" with a nearby plant or imaginary flower!

FUN CHALLENGES

Would You Rather

Question: "Eat only spicy food for a week or eat only sour food for a week?"

Challenge:

If you chose spicy food – make the hottest face you can, as if you've just eaten something super spicy!

If you chose sour food – act out the sourest face you can make, like you just bit into a lemon!

Would You Rather

Question: "Have eyebrows that grow one inch longer every day or eyelashes that fall out every time you blink?"

Challenge:

If you chose the growing eyebrows – use your hands to mime having super-long eyebrows blowing in the wind!

If you chose the falling eyelashes – close your eyes and dramatically pretend to "blink" while losing fake "eyelashes" in an over-the-top way.

FUN CHALLENGES

Would You Rather

Question: "Have super strength or super speed?"

Challenge:

If you chose super strength – flex your muscles and strike a superhero pose like you're lifting something super heavy!

If you chose super speed – run in place as fast as you can for 15 seconds, showing off your "super speed!

Would You Rather

Question: "Only be able to eat food that is green or only eat food that is purple?"

Challenge:

If you chose green food – list as many green foods as you can in 10 seconds without stopping!

If you chose purple food – describe what a day of eating only purple foods would look like (including any weird ones you can think of).

FUN CHALLENGES

Would You Rather

Question: "Be able to teleport anywhere instantly or be able to fly, but only 10 feet above the ground?"

Challenge:

If you chose teleporting – close your eyes, snap your fingers, and pretend you're in your dream destination. Describe where you "teleported" to!

If you chose flying – stretch your arms out like wings and "fly" around the room in circles for 15 seconds!

Would You Rather

Question: "Have to always talk like a robot or always laugh like a witch?"

Challenge:

If you chose robot talk – say the alphabet or count to 10 in your best robot voice!

If you chose witch laugh – give your loudest, silliest witch laugh and hold it for as long as you can!

FUN CHALLENGES

Would You Rather

Question: "Have to wear a funny hat every day or wear mismatched shoes every day?"

Challenge:

If you chose the funny hat – pretend you're wearing the silliest hat ever and walk around proudly as if it's the best hat in the world!

If you chose mismatched shoes – walk around as if your shoes are totally different sizes, and show off your unique style!

Would You Rather

Question: "Have the ability to make any food taste like chocolate or the ability to make any drink taste like soda?"

Challenge:

If you chose chocolate-flavored food – describe the weirdest food you'd turn into chocolate flavor (broccoli? spaghetti?).

If you chose soda-flavored drinks – take a pretend sip of the most unusual drink you can think of and react as if it just turned into your favorite soda!

Is This Really the End? Or Just the Beginning? 🚀

Congratulations! You've made it through a maze of the weirdest questions, the wildest choices, and the funniest challenges! You survived! And maybe, just maybe, you discovered a few things about yourself (and your friends) that will stick with you... or at least until the next hangout! 🎉

This book wasn't about choosing "peanut butter or jelly" – it was about something much bigger! Every time you answered a question about unicorns, dragons, life without the internet, or time travel, you were showing the world your unique take on life. Who knew that such crazy choices could say so much about us? 😛

A Few Words About You (Yes, YOU!):

If you chose "shouting instead of whispering," it's clear that you're brave, bold, and not afraid to be noticed! 🔊

If you opted for "always having greasy hair" – courage and humor must be your middle names! 😄

And if you'd trade your lunch for an endless supply of fries... well, we know who the real snack lover is here. 

So What's Next? 🚀

Just because you're closing this book doesn't mean the adventure ends. Actually, this is just the start of more laughs, more questions, and even weirder choices that you can now create on your own! Isn't life kind of like one endless game of "Would You Rather?" And hey, who says you have to stop playing? 

Here are a few ideas for what to do next:

Host a "Crazy Question Night" with friends! Make up your own "Would You Rather" questions and add some wild challenges. Who knows, maybe you'll invent the craziest question in the world!

Create a "Book of Weird Answers"! Jot down your funniest answers (and your friends' too) – in a few years, they'll be priceless!

Organize a "Challenge Day" – a day of dares and fun! Choose a few challenges from this book and run them in "real life!" Give your friends 30 minutes to complete as many fun tasks as possible.

Think about your choices – what if they were real? For example, what would life actually be like without a phone or in one neon outfit all year? You never know, some choices might hide cool ideas!

A Few Last Words...

Would you rather that books were always serious, or that they made you laugh until your sides hurt? Exactly! Life is a game, and every chance to laugh is golden. So hold on to your sense of humor, have fun, make weird choices, and remember – not all questions in life have just two answers. Sometimes, there's a third option... but only if you've got a pack of fries and a unicorn wearing sunglasses by your side! 😎 🌈 🍟

Thank you for choosing to go on this adventure with us. Here's to tons of laughs, joy, and... strange choices in your future! Now go ahead and close this book, but leave the door wide open for the next adventure waiting just around the corner.

Until the next big choice, my friend! 👋 ✨